Your Name In Print

A Teen's Guide To Getting Published

The only writer's guide written by teens for teens

**Danielle Dunn
& Jessica Dunn**

Copyright ©1997 by Danielle Dunn and Jessica Dunn

ISBN 1-882664-22-1

Prufrock Press   Post Office Box 8813
Waco, Texas 76714-8813
1-800-998-2208

   2

Table of Contents

Acknowledgments

We would especially like to thank our publisher Joel McIntosh for taking a chance on our book, and our editor Stephanie Stout for the countless hours of work she put into preparing the manuscript and final book for publication. Also, thanks to the rest of the staff at Prufrock Press for their efforts. A special thanks to our parents, Kathy and Bryan Dunn, and our relatives for their enthusiasm and support. We appreciate the encouragement from our English teachers, Pam Brownshadel, Anita Nance, and Jan Knox, and thank them for teaching us the process of ratiocination as it is described in this book.

Prologue

How many times have you heard that things take time, that you're not old enough to do this or that? We've heard it often enough, but when it came to writing, we didn't listen. Neither should you. Even though there were (and still are) almost no books on how young people can write for publication, we persisted.

Our story started at a Texas ranch. For one reason or another, the George Ranch in Richmond held a gathering of authors who sat at tables to sell books that they had written. We went to get autographs, but ended up with a start on our writing careers. When we expressed an interest in writing, Mrs. Ethel Evey, one of the authors, promised to send us a list of magazines that publish work by children. This really excited us because the only magazines we had heard of didn't take work from "amateur" teens. Mrs. Evey warned us that the list was very short and so old that many of the magazines may have gone out of business, but we didn't care.

For some time even after receiving the list, we went to the library three times a week looking for more markets. This sparked our part-time, no-pay "careers," so to speak, that have been going on since 1992. We selected a few magazines and started submitting our work to them. From there, our teenage writing "careers" simply took off.

Jessica has received 13 acceptances and Danielle has received 15. We have published our work in three magazines: *Creative Kids*, *Merlyn's Pen*, and *Young Authors' Magazine Anthologies* (YAM). The acceptances at these magazines consist of several puzzles and several poems each, as well as one article we wrote together for *Creative Kids*. We have also each had puzzles printed in books called *Brain Twisters!* (Prufrock Press, 1995), and *The World's Greatest Brain Bogglers* (Prufrock Press, 1996). And then, of course, there is this book itself.

So here it is: a publishing guide just for teens that comes straight from the minds of teens!

Writing the Write Way

The Write Necessities

Every writer has a different idea of the perfect way to write. The key is to develop an awareness of your own creative needs. When you write, it's important to be comfortable. Otherwise, how are you supposed to concentrate? Since all people have different definitions of comfort, you must decide what you need, then get it. How do you do your best work? If you prefer to do rough drafts by talking into a tape recorder, buy one. Make sure you have it and several tapes at your fingertips whenever you could possibly need them. If you can't write without super-sharp pencils, try to get an electric pencil sharpener. Make whatever investments are necessary within reason; they may pay off in bylines later.

We both use spiral notebooks to scratch down and refine our ideas. Many of our published puzzles originated in our notebooks. We strongly encourage this sort of "writing ideas" journal, as it is very helpful. You can set one up with dividers, creating separate sections for story  ideas, poem ideas, puzzles, etc. Your dividers will be labeled according to what types of works you create. If you don't ever write poetry, don't make a divider for it. There should be one divider (section) per type.

You may want to get a college-ruled spiral in order to save space. Whatever you do, get a thick one to hold your many ideas. Even if you do your writing on a computer, it's a good idea to have something to carry with you everywhere. You never know when that flash of inspiration will hit you!

Many professionals also keep journals or diaries. Writing about your daily experiences is a great way to practice writing and may open doors to future topics. If you wanted to write an article on a unique vacation, for instance, you could use some of what you wrote in your journal. Entries in these are most often written during special events or soon afterwards. If you go back later to read it, the journal will remind you of the little things that you've probably long forgotten. In a journal, feelings are described in such detail that if you quote some of the entry in your article, it will be more intimate. The readers will feel as if they were really there with you. Such "inside" looks are very desirable in writing.

In fact, Agatha Christie was once asked how she came up with the exotic settings for her mysteries. She responded that she "wrote what she knew." Most were from experiences she actually had — even if the murders were not.

The Write Tips

It should be noted before beginning that writing comes in all different forms. You've probably been learning in English class about how to write essays and stories, but that isn't the end of it. Not even close. Writing can also be a math book that teaches math in an insightful, easy-to-learn way or a history book explaining how to memorize the two-letter abbreviations of every state. There is poetry, news writing, technical writing, such as what's listed above, how-to, or literary writings like stories and essays.

 8

Even now you may think you're a good story writer, and that's what you want to be. That's great, but don't close your mind to all other options. Try other writing forms. You just may find a niche that suits you even better. To start just read the "Write Tips" below and apply them to other forms of writing.

Be observant. Pay close attention to the world around you, your environment. Note how the tree branches sway slightly in the breeze. Listen to the patterns of the birds' chirping. Hear and feel the rhythm of the joggers on the street. Become a people watcher. Observe any unusual behavior or funny occurrences. Just stay alert and use your senses. You may be surprised. Often ideas for stories, essays, and especially poems are inspired by a small detail of nature or a funny happening around you. Observe your world and elaborate on its wonders and small miracles in your writing!

Just write. Get your ideas out on paper. Don't worry about grammar (yet). Don't worry about punctuation or spelling. Don't think about your handwriting. Don't even bother writing in complete sentences, if necessary!

Just pour out those ideas, those special thoughts, those interesting phrases and details. Get them on paper before you forget them! Write now; think later! You may even carry a portable tape recorder to tape interesting observations. (Note: Be sure to write down or record every single idea you have, even if you feel immediately that you will never use it. Sometimes even the worst ideas may be improved later, or they may spark new and better ideas. After all, one idea can lead to another. You never know. Therefore, it is advisable to write down all of your creative thoughts.)

Write what you know and what you want to know. Besides creating poems and stories based on your observations, you may write works based on events or experiences. You should "Write what you know." It wouldn't serve you too well to be a romance writer if you've never been in a romantic relationship. However, it could also be said that you should write what you want to know. Do some research at your local library, then write about what you read. Chances are there are other young people out there who have the same interests. Sure, you may be one of only 50 kids in America with a passion for knowing how paint is made, but give it a shot anyway. Anything is possible.

The most important thing to know about your topic is this: is experience really required in order to create an informative, accurate work? If so, you will need to write what you know and be sure to have experience before you create the work. If not, extensive research should give you enough knowledge to make your point. This is what journalistic writing is all about. News reporters do research and then write what they have learned all the time.

Rewrite and rewrite your work. Now that your ideas are on paper, it's time to get a little more picky. You may have written your ideas in a nonsense fashion. Each individual idea makes sense, but they do not flow together as a whole. Rearrange them until you are satisfied with your work. Change around those words and phrases. Get everything worded just as you want it, then add a few transitional phrases to connect the pieces and make them flow together. Elaborate. Write and write and write again. Go through your work. Change it. Get it right.

Edit your work to correct grammar, spelling, and punctuation. Use ratiocination (see "Nothing's

Perfect the First Time Around"). Look up possibly misspelled words in the dictionary.

Once you've finished all of this, type your manuscript on a computer or typewriter and print a clean copy. Have some people read and critique it, preferably people from the age group that you are aiming for as an audience for your work. If it's meant to be read by young teenagers, for example, have a young teenager critique it. Then seriously consider following the suggestions of your critics.

If their suggestions sound logical and reasonable to you, if they sound like good ideas, follow them. If not, follow your own instincts. The most important thing is to have confidence in your work. Revise your work until you are comfortable with it.

When, at last, you are satisfied with your manuscript, send it off to a publication. Hopefully the editors will like it as much as you do. Once again, good luck getting an acceptance! It's a wonderful feeling!

Nothing's Perfect the First Time Around

Ratiocination is a special editing process best used for prose (fiction or nonfiction) that we learned about in the sixth, eighth, and ninth grades. It involves a few different colors so you might want to get several markers, colored pencils, or highlighters before you start.

First, find six different colors of markers and use each to write one word in the margin of your paper. These words are "who," "what," "where," "when," "why," and "how." Each word should be written in a different color. Next, use each corresponding color to underline or highlight the answers to each question in your manuscript. For example, if you wrote "who" in yellow, underline or highlight the names and descriptions of characters in your story in yellow. The words in the margin are all questions that must be answered in every work of fiction or nonfiction. If you lack the answer to any question, edit your work until you have it.

Then you may wish to print a clean, corrected copy of your manuscript. This is a reason why a computer is helpful; you can make any necessary changes easily and print a fresh copy. The reason that we suggest you print a new copy is that when you try to perform every step of ratiocination on one sheet of paper, it becomes messy.

Once you have checked for these major parts of a piece, edit for content. Make sure that you have included all desired and necessary information in your article. If you are writing a story, underline the first two sentences and study them carefully. If they are creative and intriguing, you have a good opening that will hook the reader and encourage him or her to keep reading. If not, you have a weak opening and should change it.

Also, check to make sure that the story flows. Be sure to have an introduction to the conflict, events leading up to a climax, and events leading to a solution to the problem and conclusion. You may wish to have a few of your peers or family members read your piece and make comments.

The next step is to check your wording and sentence length. Begin by choosing two different colors. Take the first one and use it to underline the entire first sentence. Pick up the other and underline the entire second sentence with it. Continue alternating back and forth until you have underlined every sentence in your paper.

Once you have completed this, study the underlined sentences. The colored underlining makes it much easier to observe the lengths of your sentences. Try to make them vary. Edit your work to achieve a balance between the numbers of long and short sentences. When all of your sentences are short, the paper doesn't flow well. If you make them all long the paper seems to go on endlessly.

Find a third colored marker. Use it to put brackets around the first word of every sentence in your manuscript. Then look at each of these words to see if you have used a word to start a sentence more than once on each page.

For example, if you used the word "she" to start more than one sentence on a page, you should consider changing it. Count how many times you used it on the page and try to cut that number in half when you edit. Do this for each page individually. Try to use a word only once on one page if possible; however, you may use it again on the next.

A fourth color of marker should be used for the next step. Circle all of your "to be" verbs, such as "am," "was," "were," etc. "To be" verbs can be very important to a sentence, but they begin to seem useless and redundant when overused. They also make your work passive rather than active. Therefore, it is best to keep them to a minimum. Try to reword your sentences to eliminate a few when you edit. Cut the number you have in half if you can.

You may also want to underline the words "get," "got," "very," "real," "a lot," "good," "bad," "nice," and "great" in a fifth color and try to reword them. Like "to be" verbs, these are overused and should be avoided whenever possible.

Ratiocination Example

[I] gripped the reins tightly so as not to fall off then made an attempt to calm Betsy. [When] there (was) no longer any danger of being thrown out of the saddle, I turned to face the girl with a defiant look.

[“Why] did you do that? [Either] one of us could have (been) hurt, and now thanks to you, we'll probably (be) late for the train.”

Check to make sure that you have worded your story in a way that makes sense. Check your grammar; most importantly, make sure the subjects and verbs agree with each other (if your subject is plural, your verb must be plural also, etc.). Make sure that your spelling is correct, too. If you are using a word processor, you may use the spell-check function to do this. Be careful with spell-check, though. If you accidentally print the word “their,” for example, rather than the needed “there,” the spell-check won't catch it (both are correctly spelled words). You need to look your work over yourself as well after spell-checking it. Some word-processing programs also have a similar grammar-check function. If yours does, use it. Still, it is always best to check your own work as well.

Finally, you should give your work an overall proof-reading. Check to be sure you wrote in complete sentences and eliminated all run-ons. Begin each sentence with a capital letter, of course, and conclude it with the correct end punctuation. Make sure that you capitalized letters and used commas properly within sentences. Be sure to indent each paragraph. For convenience, you may wish to use the following proofreading marks.

- ℘ Delete a letter, word, phrase, sentence, paragraph, or punctuation mark.
- — Draw a line through the letter, word, etc., and write a new one above it. This mark, therefore, is used to change letters, words, phrases, sentences, etc.
- ^ Add a letter, word, phrase, sentence, etc.
- ⌃ Add a comma.
- ⊗ Add a period.
- / Change to lower case.
- ≡ Change to upper case (capital).
- ⌐ Start over here with a new paragraph; indent.
- ∽ Switch letters, words, or punctuation marks.
- ⱽ Add quotation marks

An example of a paragraph edited with these marks:

When you are proofreading a paragraph of your writing sure be to use these marks. They help you a lot ⊗ every time I go and write a story, I use them to edit my Work.
⌐Although I really don't enjoy editing (it is rather tedious), I always *often* tell myself, ⱽIf you want an acceptance, Danielle, you will edit your work!ⱽ

Once you have finished editing, get back on your computer and make the changes you have marked.

Important Note to the Reader: See the appendix in the back of this book for a list of references that will help you to improve your writing.

Does Making Puzzles Puzzle You?

Many magazines, including *Creative Kids* and *Merlyn's Pen*, accept puzzles for publication in addition to stories, poems, essays, and book reviews. In fact, puzzles may very well be the fastest route to your first byline (editors can never seem to get enough of them). Plus, in our opinion, they are as fun and as challenging to make as they are to solve.

If you have never made puzzles before, you may want to start with word searches and crosswords. They are not too difficult to create, making them very good for practice.

To create a word search, pick 20 or so words related to the same theme. This theme, if you choose to submit these "practice puzzles," should probably relate to that of the magazine you are aiming at. Arrange the words so that they connect together and cross each other like the words in a crossword. Then simply fill in the spaces between and around these words with randomly picked letters to form a large square or rectangular block of letters. Below this block, type the words to search for.

Crosswords are made the same way; at least the first step is the same. Arrange the words so that they connect and cross. This time, however, you must number each word and write a clue to go with it. Be sure that the clues suit the age group of the magazine you are submitting your crossword to. For example, if the readers are rather young, make the clues a little more obvious. Don't just give the answers away, but do not make the clues confusing or otherwise difficult to figure out. The language should be clear and simple. If the readers are older, feel free to challenge them a little more.

Now you have the solution to the puzzle. From this you must form the puzzle itself by replacing each letter in each word with a small empty square. We have a computer program, called Formtool, which we find to be extremely helpful in constructing puzzles. If you have such a program, by all means use it (you may even have a program that specializes in this sort of thing). If not, you will have to construct the puzzle by hand. We recommend you use a ruler and graph paper to do this.

You may also create mazes for publication. Because these have very little uniformity, you will have to use your imagination. Sit down with a pencil and ruler and draw some lines. See what you come up with. You may find it helpful to solve mazes and look at examples. If you submit a maze, make sure that it has dark, thick lines so it will reproduce well in the publication.

Mazes, word searches, and crossword puzzles appear often in magazines. However, we prefer more difficult, thought-provoking puzzles. So we submit logic puzzles instead. They are far more unique and provide readers with a greater challenge. Also, we've been told that editors really like them.

We are not experts on logic puzzles, but we have had eight of ours published, four in *Creative Kids* and four in *Merlyn's Pen*. We've also been published in two puzzle books from Prufrock Press, *Brain Twisters!* and the *World's Greatest Brain Bogglers*. Logic puzzles remind us of riddles. Using a set of clues and an answer chart or diagram, provided by the creator, the reader attempts to solve the puzzle.

Logic puzzles usually involve matching certain items. For instance, these factors may be four people, four hobbies, and four favorite subjects in school. The reader would match each person to his or her favorite hobby and favorite school subject using the clues and the diagram, then record the answers in the diagram or answer chart.

Some clues are very straightforward and give the reader a definite match ("Jamie's hobby is skating"). However, don't use too many of these or the puzzle will be far too easy. The better clues allow the reader to use the process of elimination (according to the clues, Jamie can't have this, this, or this favorite hobby so she must have this one, the only choice left). These clues require the reader, or puzzle-solver, to make inferences and figure things out. That, after all, is the fun of a logic puzzle. Be reasonable, however. Your puzzle should again suit the age group of the magazine's readers. If the readers are younger, you may use more of the straight-forward clues; however, if they are older, be sure to use more of the process-of-elimination clues to challenge them more. Also, the more factors or items to be matched up, the harder the puzzle will be.

During lunch, Kathy and her four friends sat together at their usual table and discussed their favorite subjects. Each was willing to listen to the others, but was most eager to tell about her own favorite class. Each girl had a different drink, and no two girls had the same favorite subject. Using the clues and diagram below, determine where each girl sat, what her favorite subject was, and what drink she had that day.

1. The two girls on the south side of the table have sodas (with different brand names), while those on the north side have more nutritious drinks.
2. Kathy and Danielle are seated next to each other on the north side of the table.
3. The two girls who like science and math are seated on the south side of the table.
4. Rachel is in seat 5. The girl whose favorite subject is English is seated next to Rachel.
5. The girl who especially enjoys health class is drinking milk.
6. Danielle does not like health class. She does, however, drink orange juice everyday at lunch.
7. Rachel loves history class. Kim loves science.
8. Jessica is drinking a Dr Pepper™. Kim is in seat 2.
9. The girls' drinks are Dr Pepper™, Diet Coke™, apple juice, milk, and orange juice.

	English	Science	Math	Health	History	Dr Pepper	Diet Coke	Apple Juice	Milk	Orange Juice
Kathy										
Danielle										
Jessica										
Kim										
Rachel										

Logic puzzles should include an introduction. This paragraph explains the puzzle and tells the reader (puzzle-solver) what to do in order to solve it. The introduction is often in the form of a story and describes the items or factors to be matched up. Always include this introductory paragraph in your logic puzzles so that they will make sense to the reader. Be very specific in explaining how to work the puzzle or the reader won't get past the first clue.

Logic puzzles are most convenient to solve with the use of a special chart. We think it should be called a mind-bender box, although quite possibly it has no name. As the clues are used, Xs and dots are marked in the chart. The factors of your puzzle, for example, may be the hobby, favorite subject, favorite food, and favorite rock group of each person. List the names of the people across the top of a piece of paper. Down the left side, list choices for each factor. (Study the example of a logic puzzle on page 18). Look closely at the mind-bender box; this will help you to create your own.) Draw lines down and across to create boxes where different factor choices intersect (see example). Then if a clue states that a person didn't have a certain hobby, the reader would find the box where the person's column and hobbies row intersect. The reader would put an X in that box. Dots mark correct match-ups.

By studying examples of logic puzzles, we figured out for ourselves how to create them and what the clues should be like. The methods we devised for creation were slightly different for each of us. One is to first decide your factors and the choices for each one, as well as the people or animals to match the choices to. Then create your chart and the introductory paragraph that explains the puzzle. Last, write your clues. As you write each one, mark any applicable Xs or dots in the chart.

Continue to make clues until you fill in the entire chart. In reality, this method involves solving a puzzle as you create it.

You may have seen a few plexors in magazines, in books of puzzles, or at school. These puzzles are little word and picture games. An example is:

---
house

PRAIRIE

The solution to this puzzle is "Little House on the Prairie," the title of a popular series by Laura Ingalls Wilder and a TV show. To create such puzzles can be a bit tricky. One of the easiest ways to go about it is to start by thinking of book titles, common phrases or slogans, etc. Then think of a way to depict these using a few words or drawings. In the example above, "little house" was shown by writing the word "house" very small; this was placed on top of the word "prairie" to finish out the book title.

You can make these puzzles using only words, or a mix of words and drawings, but it is not a great idea to make any using only drawings. If you do use just words, try to use very few and be sure that the size and/or position of the words have an effect on the solution as they did in the example above. If you use too many words, the puzzles will be too easy.

If you use a mix of words and drawings, try to achieve an equal balance between them. For instance, if you are trying to depict the state name Oklahoma, it would not be advisable to draw an oak tree and then write "lahoma." This would give the answer away because Oklahoma is the only state name with that ending. Try to add more drawings. You could draw an oak tree, write "la," draw a house, and then write "a."

If you plan to submit such puzzles, be sure to send a collection of about 10 as one submission. They are too small to be submitted individually.

There are many more types of puzzles, word games, and even riddles (such as "Who Am I?" riddles) that you can submit for publication. When it comes to puzzle submissions, almost anything goes. (After all, no one ever seems to get enough of them, including editors. This great need for puzzle contributions also, as said before, makes them a good place to break into publishing.) You might go to the grocery store and look for puzzle collections or magazines full of variety puzzles, riddles, games, etc. Study these different types of puzzles and solve a few of them. You may learn about more kinds to make, and you may invent new ways of making them. It really doesn't matter how you go about creating the puzzles, as long as your finished products have the necessary puzzle elements. (If your finished logic puzzle has no clues, for example, you cannot call it a logic puzzle.) As always, it is easier to start by solving puzzles. After that you can use your knowledge to make a few of your own.

Note: Once you become a more experienced puzzle-maker, you may want to experiment with inventing new types of puzzles. (After all, at one point somebody made up the logic puzzle type, etc.) This way you can make up your own rules and be truly creative. Don't limit yourself to making puzzles that fall into a known category!

The Starting Line

So You're Hungry for a Byline

You've decided to become a published author. We suppose you're eager to get the address of a publication, write something, stuff it in an envelope, put a stamp on it, send it off, and wait for a glowing acceptance letter. Unfortunately, things just aren't that simple. If you care to reap the rewards for your efforts, you must begin at the beginning.

You will need a few materials if you want to be a writer. The most important tool is a computer. It is most convenient to own a computer with a word-processing program. However, you may have access to a word-processor at your school, a local library or college, at your parent's office, or even at a friend's house if he or she has one.

If you have access only to a typewriter, that will work. However, typewriters can be inconvenient because you must keep a hard copy of everything you send off. Also, many editors prefer to receive accepted material on a disk to save them the time of retyping your manuscript. Being able to provide this can sometimes make the difference between acceptance and rejection.

Another good reason to use a computer is so you have a backup copy in case your work gets lost in the mail (though that doesn't happen often) or you may need a new copy to send to a different publication. Also, editors often write on work, making it even more necessary that you keep extra copies. With access to a computer, you can simply store your work on a disk, call it up, and print a fresh copy without retyping. If you don't have a typewriter or a computer, talk to your parents.

Once you have your supplies taken care of, look at some of the publications in the back of this book. Along with the addresses, we have listed some information about each. Go to your local library and enlist the help of a reference librarian. He or she can help you explore even more options for publishing work. Resources at your library, for example, may be available to help you find local outlets for your work. Create a list of the publications you would like to begin to send work to. Make sure that you are within the required age group, and that their other characteristics conform to your liking. For example, we never submit anything to a publication whose editors don't send at least one free copy of each of the issues containing our work. Many publishers do not pay young authors; however, such free copies, called complimentary copies or contributor's copies, are usually sent. Beware of publications that require a purchase in order to publish your work!

Being published and not knowing how our work looks in print is very frustrating for us. You may not care about this however. Go with your own standards, not ours. For example, you may refuse to submit work to any magazine unless they give you a byline and print biographical information as well. You may be unwilling to wait a year for publication and will want to see your work in print after a few months. This will, however, narrow your market a good deal. Perhaps you only write poems and will not contribute at all to a magazine that doesn't accept them, or maybe you are picky about the magazine's distribution or length limits. You might even require cash payment. However, we would not recommend this standard because it would severely limit your market choices (very few children's magazines pay their contributors, although it's common with book presses).

Decide what your own needs are and stick to them. For instance, if you decide you must have a complimentary copy, but a publication's guidelines don't say that they provide one, it never hurts to ask for one. Also, you really should consider copyright agreements and rights (see "The Right to Own What You Write").

Now that you have made your list, you are ready to submit your work, right? Wrong. Next you have to get guidelines for submissions. Type up a letter that you can send to the publications on your list as a request for guidelines. Use the business letter format that you've probably learned in school (if you haven't studied this, your library should have several references on letter writing). Explain your interest in sending work to the publication; then ask that the editors send you some writer's guidelines. The following chapter has an example of a guideline request. The guidelines themselves are almost always free, but you should send a self-addressed stamp envelope (SASE) for them to mail the guidelines back to you. The guidelines will tell you what information needs to be included with each submission and the formats for your submission.

Many guidelines that we have read also say that it is necessary to read sample issues of a publication to which you wish to send your work. Often they suggest that you read not just one, but at least six months to a year's worth of back issues. These may be difficult to find unless you subscribe to the magazine yourself. Look at the library first. If it doesn't carry the magazine, try looking at a different and/or larger library in your area. If you still can't find copies, talk to some friends and see if they subscribe. You could always borrow copies from them. If your school has a subscription for the classroom, by all means take a look in the magazine. As a last resort you could order a few sample copies from the publication itself; the prices usually range from $1 to $5, and some are listed in the directory in the back of this book. You might subscribe also if you think you may like to read the magazine for your own pleasure as well as for research. However you go about it, try to find as many back issues as you can and study them thoroughly. Editors will not accept work that does not meet their needs. Follow the guidelines that they send you to the letter. Reading back issues is important as well; otherwise you won't know the audience and style of works accepted. Without this knowledge, acceptance is almost impossible.

After you receive responses to your guideline requests, study them very carefully. Be sure that when you make a submission, you follow each of the requirements for the publication you are sending to and not any other. Don't add a lot of information that was not requested. Of special importance, be sure to include all information and materials that were requested in the format requested. One exception to the "always follow the rules" rule is: send an SASE for their response even if they don't ask for one or mention it. However, if the guidelines specifically say not to send an SASE, don't bother to do it. (Some publications respond only to accepted material and, therefore, do not ask for SASEs to return rejected work.) The following chapter contains more information on how to do these things and how to format your work.

When you send your work off to a publication, be sure not to make any simultaneous submissions. This is when you send the same manuscript to more than one magazine at a time. Publications will usually request the right to be the first to publish a piece. If more than one accepts the work you will be in a bind and may not get published at all. However, do not confuse this with multiple submission, which means to send more than one manuscript in the same envelope to the same publication. Some editors discourage this, and if they do, sometimes they will tell you so in the guidelines. However, we would not advise it unless they specifically say it is OK.

Stamps will become costly when your writing career takes off. In order to save yourself some money, it is best to buy not only first-class stamps but some of the cheaper ones as well. Then you can combine stamps of different prices so that you don't spend any more money than necessary. If you take your submissions to the window at the post office they will tell you the exact amount of postage needed. Otherwise the postage chart in the back of this book will tell you how much you need to spend on each submission and each SASE if you want to send one large enough to return your manuscript.

Some magazines require that you have more than one stamp on your SASE because of the number of forms that they send with an acceptance. With these forms, the weight of the envelope will mean higher costs. However, they never say the number of stamps, just "include sufficient postage." It is wise to put on enough postage to return your manuscript. Rarely will the forms weigh more. If they do, the envelope will reach you postage due and you will have to pick it up at the post office. Never assume anything. The amount of postage you put on an SASE must be enough for an acceptance or a rejection. Just because one stamp might cover an acceptance, it doesn't mean one is enough; consider rejections as well.

Envelopes are another matter to consider. You can find general styles at your local office supply store. For guideline requests you can use normal business-size envelopes, 4⅛" x 9½". When you make submissions, however, you should never fold your manuscripts. They must be sent in manuscript envelopes, which are 9" x 12" in size. For book manuscripts, you can find manuscript boxes.

SASEs sent with submissions are ideally 6½" x 9½". Otherwise, find something similar. Again, a well stocked office supply store should have plenty to choose from. For guideline requests, use business-size SASEs, just like the outer envelopes. Always remember to enclose an SASE with anything you send to a publication, unless otherwise requested. Most of the publications you will send your work to will not respond if you don't send an envelope. (Some will not respond even if you do). Put your own postage on it, and the publication will be able to respond when it receives it with your submission. Some publications also ask that you send an SASP (self-addressed, stamped postcard) so they can notify you of receipt of your work before they evaluate it. Don't enclose one requesting that they do this for you if they don't suggest it. They probably won't use it.

Before we move on, there is one last thing that must be noted. When you write for publication, only a certain percentage of works submitted will be accepted. For the two of us this has been about 20 percent. More than likely, the more work you submit, the more work you will have published. If you intend to rack up a good deal of acceptances, send a lot of work. Send anything and everything, at least to an extent. Be sure that everything you submit is your best work.

It won't do you any good to make a 100 submissions in a year if none of them is any good. For example, Danielle started off sending everything she wrote to magazines (for the record, she only submits her best work now). She submitted almost 1½ times as many works as Jessica but has only two more acceptances. It is good to send a lot, but be a little selective about what you send.

If you send work that has the best chance of acceptance, your time and effort will be worth it. In a nutshell: write a lot, send almost everything, and quite possibly get published an amazing number of times.

It may even be worthwhile to set up a system with

yourself. Make two submissions a week, for instance, more if you can. Keep it up. Chances are if you do this you will get two responses a week, which is an awful lot of fun. Publishing is guaranteed to be a great experience for you.

Submitting to Publications — Step by Step

The Basic Steps:
1. Create the poem, story, essay, puzzle, or whatever it is you want to submit.
2. On a computer or typewriter, type the work according to the publication's desired format (according to the guidelines). Type everything else you need, also (things like a cover letter, etc.).
3. Print it all. Always use white, unlined paper.
4. Place everything in a large manuscript envelope big enough to allow you to put the work inside without folding it.
5. Enclose an SASE for a reply from the publication unless the guidelines tell you to do otherwise.
6. Seal the outer envelope (be careful never to seal the SASE), stamp it, and mail it.
7. Waiting ...
8. Waiting ...
9. And waiting!
10. The publication responds!
11. Start over with a new piece.

If Accepted:
1. Get very excited!
2. Fill out and sign any forms that the publisher has sent (but be sure to read them first!). If you are a minor (under 18), your parent or legal guardian must also sign the forms.
3. Make copies of the forms for your files and mail

the forms back to the publisher as soon as possible.

4. Now, get very excited again.
5. Make copies of the work and give them to your friends and family.
6. Wait a few months to a year (sometimes longer) for the magazine to publish your work.
7. Get all excited again! No matter how long, it's always worth the wait!

If Rejected:
1. Don't get discouraged.
2. Edit the work, especially according to the editor's suggestions (if any).
3. Try again at that publication or send the edited work elsewhere.
4. Remember that there's always hope!
5. Look forward to a possible acceptance!

Good Luck!

Letter and Manuscript Formats

This is one of the most important sections in this book. Unfortunately, it is probably the most tedious as well. We will try to make it as brief as possible, for your sake, but you must remember the importance of this information.

Guideline requests are essential. You must follow a publication's guidelines explicitly in order to submit to it properly. Many editors will automatically reject work that does not follow their guidelines exactly. In your request for guidelines, you must be polite (ask, don't demand!). Also, use the editor's name (but never address the editor by his or her first name) in your greeting if at all possible. (If you found the publication listed in a market guide, the editor's name will probably be included. Our directory also lists the editors' names for all magazine and book publishers, but it's a good idea to check the most recent issue anyway. Otherwise you may look in the beginning of a sample copy of the magazine on the masthead. The masthead is simply a list of all the staff that work for a publication. If you can't find the name, call the magazine and ask to whom work should be addressed.) As in all business letters, never use exclamation points. An example of a typical guideline request follows.

Your Name
Your Street Address
Your City, State Zip Code
The Date

Name of publication
Street Address of publication
City, State Zip Code of publication

Dear Editor (use name if possible) :

I am interested in submitting my work to your publication, and I am requesting a copy of your writer's guidelines. If you have any available, please send me a copy. I have enclosed an SASE for your convenience. Thank you very much.

Sincerely,

Your Name

A cover letter is also necessary. One of these must be included with every submission to a publication. In this letter you should introduce yourself, give the title of your work, and summarize the work very briefly. It is very important in a cover letter that you address the editor by name. It shows you've done your research (see above). Be polite and thank the editors for their consideration of your work. An example of a cover letter is shown below.

Your Name
Your Street Address
Your City, State Zip Code
The Date

Name of publication
Street Address of publication
City, State Zip Code of publication

Dear Name of Editor:

My name is (your name). With this letter I have enclosed a copy of my (poem, story, essay, puzzle), titled (title of work). It is about (summarize work in this sentence). I hope you enjoy reading it. Please consider it for publication in (name of publication). Thank you.

Sincerely,
(Handwrite your name)
(type your name)

Some magazines, such as *Spring Tides*, require that you enclose a "promise of originality" letter with each submission. (Be sure to check the guidelines to see if they want one). This letter, signed and dated by your parent or guardian, states and promises that your work is original (not copied) and that only you created the work. An example:

Date

This is to verify that the enclosed work, [Title of work] is an original work by my [son/daughter/child], [your name]. Thank you.

Sincerely,

Signature of parent/guardian

Magazines vary in their format requirements, but most of them agree on some universal rules.

- First and foremost, label every page with your name.
- Secondly, always double-space your work (skip a space between each typed line).
- Also, you must left-justify your manuscript. Left-justified means that the words are lined up at the left margin but not on the right. (Fully justified is another acceptable type of format meaning that both margins are lined up).
- Most publications will also ask that you leave at least a one-inch margin on all sides of each page.

Beyond this, it depends on the publication. (Be sure to follow their instructions). Below is a sample manuscript format:

Your Name
Your School
Your Address
School Address
Your Phone Number
School Phone
Your Age and Grade
Your Teacher's Name

Title

Manuscript Body

On the following pages, if any:

Your Name   Title   Page Number

Manuscript Body (continued)

For poems, the work may be double- or single-spaced and centered or left-justified, whichever the publication tells you to do.

Remember to always request guidelines from a publication before submitting to it. Follow their directions for manuscript formats very carefully. At the top of the first page of your manuscript, type whatever personal information they want from you as a contributor, unless otherwise instructed (some magazines may prefer that you put this information on a separate piece of paper or index card). Good luck!

Writing is a Profession — Act Professional!

Right now you may believe that using pretty stationary, colored paper, or bright envelopes is a good way to impress an editor. This, however, isn't at all true. It's important that you keep things simple. Don't be cute, but be polite whenever you write or call an editor. It's the best way to keep your place in the publishing world. Below are some of the fundamentals of etiquette and professionalism.

Always address the editor by name, if possible, but never use his or her first name in your salutation. As mentioned in the section on letter and manuscript formats, one of the most important aspects of professionalism is knowing an editor's name. Using it is better than "Dear Editor" even as early as sending off for guideline requests. Using names is absolutely necessary when you make submissions. If you found the names of the publications you want to send work to in the directory at the back of this book, you'll notice that the editors' names are listed there; problem solved.

The same will probably go for any other guide that you may use. However, if names aren't given, try to find the magazine at the library. The masthead near the front will have the names. If the magazine isn't at the library, the guideline requests will have to be written using "Dear Editor."

Once you receive the guidelines, read them carefully to make sure the publication is right for you. If you still have an interest in sending your work there, order a sample copy from the publication itself and look at the masthead. Even if you already knew one or two names, it's always nice to know more. *Merlyn's Pen* has a lot of editors, several of whom have reviewed our work for publication.

Phone calls are another matter to consider. Try to take it easy on them. In the directory, we have listed the phone numbers of many of the editorial offices of publications. However, the point of this is not so that you can call your editor and chat for several hours about anything that comes to mind. Editors are very busy people.

Most correspondence should be by mail. There are a few cases, however, when it is simply more convenient to call, and when it won't be inconvenient for the editor. For example, *Merlyn's Pen* has a toll-free number that you can call when you have questions or comments. If no one is available, there is an answering machine for you to leave your number.

Try not to call about the status of your work even if a response is overdue. We know it's frustrating, but again editors are very busy people. Things happen once in a while. Besides, if you call an editor about a manuscript the editor will probably have to keep you on hold for a minute or two and go dig for it. This can be very inconvenient for both people, especially if your call is long distance and not toll-free.

The bills will skyrocket if you get into a habit of calling. It upsets the editors, anyway; send inquiries on the status of manuscripts through the mail. When you do call with questions, be brief. You can even write out word for word what you will say if it makes you feel less nervous about talking to an adult you don't really know.

Some general guidelines you should follow regardless of an editor's written guidelines include:

🖊 Use 20-pound bond, white, unlined, 8½" x 11" paper. Don't use erasable bond or onion skin paper. Be sure to print only on one side, using a simple style of type (no script; nothing fancy, just ordinary print.

- Be sure it is a normal type size, too — nothing enormous or microscopic. Double-space everything.

- Don't use paper clips. You can staple your manuscript or use a binder clip if it's too thick. Never staple the cover letter to anything.

- Don't use folders or report covers for the manuscript. Don't handwrite on work or make other marks. Go easy on the whiteout. Some publications prefer that you send more than one copy of a submission. Be sure to do this if the guidelines tell you to. Otherwise, just send one copy.

- Avoid using stationery. Double-space letters and use a business letter format (see the previous section). Always be courteous and brief.

- Write neatly on white or brown envelopes. Don't use colors, pictures, stickers, or tape. Basically, don't be cute.

- Use labels or stamps if you have them. If you can, get a stamp or labels with your name and address on them. It takes less time than printing your return address on submission envelopes and your address on SASEs. It's also neater for the post office and very professional looking. Take a look through your junk mail. Chances are you'll find an order form for stamps or labels. They' re very inexpensive. If you do get labels, make sure they are white with a simple printing font.

If your manuscript is rejected, never send the same copy to a different publication. Most likely a rejected copy will be folded, worn, or written upon by the editor. This makes it very obvious to the new editor that your manuscript was previously submitted elsewhere and rejected (not a good selling point). Sending an old copy also looks very unprofessional. Instead, send a fresh copy printed from your computer, or a clean photocopy (unless the original was written upon).

The Right to Own What You Write

Rights, in a nutshell, deal with the ownership of a creative work. As the creator of the work, you own the rights to it unless you assign them to someone else. If accepted, you will probably want to know to whom your work will belong after publication.

Rights situations vary. Some publications use one time use rights, which allow the publication to print your work once and afterward the rights revert back to you. Under this agreement, you can have that work published elsewhere if you wish. Within one time use rights are first time rights. This term means that the publication asking for these rights wants to print the work once for the first time anywhere in the world. Many publications ask for first time rights with reprint rights. Reprint rights allow the publication to use your work again for anthologies or other projects by the same publisher. Other publications take all rights, which means that once they accept your work and you sign a contract, they own it. They can then print it as many times as they wish anywhere in the world in any format, and you cannot submit that work to any other publication without their permission. Often, however, publications for children which request all rights will allow the student to self-publish or publish in a school publication. You may wish to ask about this situation.

Even so, you may not care for the all rights situation, because legally it means no longer owning your own work. You do not have to accept the publication's rights requests, but you will jeopardize your chance at publication if you don't. Further, if you are uncomfortable with their requests, you can ask them to modify the contract. The other option, of course, is simply not to submit your work there at all.

Rights are a legal issue. Magazine editors will most likely send you one or two official forms and contracts to sign if they accept your work. You should receive a license of copyright form. If you do not sign this form giving your permission for the magazine to publish your work, they won't publish it at all. (Without the signed forms, they do not legally have the right to use your work.) Your parent or guardian must also sign the form if you are under the age of 18. By signing this form, you relinquish the particular rights to your work that are specified in the contract. Once you've done this, the matter is closed, whether the publication uses the piece or not. (*Highlights*, for example, takes all rights on accepted works without guarantee of publication.) You may want to make sure the publication is definitely going to print the piece before signing.

Also, the publication may send you a promise of originality form, which you must fill out and sign. This states that you, and only you, wrote the work. Otherwise, the editors are not protected in the case of plagiarism.

Don't worry too much about these forms. Usually they are pretty easy to understand. Whenever the language or wording is too complex, you can contact the magazine's editors and ask them to explain it to you. Just follow the instructions on your acceptance letter and you should do fine.

Although rights and copyright are the same thing in most cases, there are some important issues specific to copyright. If you have rights to your work, you own it and can submit it elsewhere. Copyright is a legal protection against the unauthorized publication of your work. A copyright is automatically placed on a creative work as soon as it is created (as the author or artist, you hold the copyright). Therefore the work is protected by law against plagiarism. It is illegal for anyone to copy your work or a piece of it without your permission. It is also illegal for someone to claim that your work is theirs.

Copyright becomes very important when your work is published. When this happens, the copyright holder may change. If you have a book published, it will probably be copyrighted and registered at the copyright office in your name by the publisher, and, therefore, you will hold it. However, if your work is published in a magazine, the publication will probably hold the copyright to the actual printed material. This is because publications place (and register) copyrights on their magazines as collective works. Be aware that even if you do retain the copyright of your individual work, the publication still owns the copyright of the issue in which it appeared. Therefore, you may not use their layouts, formats, or graphics without their permission. You may not use photocopies of the work or any graphic designs they may add.

If your work has been previously published, and you would like to resubmit it, you must first check that you retain the rights to it and that the new publication will consider previously published work. If so, be sure to mention in your new cover letter (see "Letter and Manuscript Formats") that the work has been published before and where.

NOTE: If you insist upon retaining the rights to your work (so that you can submit it elsewhere), ask the publication, before you even submit to it, what rights it requests for accepted work.

For a complete explanation of the most common rights situations, look in the glossary.

What Now?

Decisions, Decisions!

When it comes to making submissions, you have a couple of major decisions to make. Again, you will have to choose which way to go according to your values and what works best for you. Below, the benefits of each choice are explained, so that you may weigh them carefully and make the decisions most beneficial to you.

When it comes to marketing your work, you have two basic options; you could either select a few publications (perhaps five) and submit all of your work to them, or you may choose to submit to as many different publications as possible. The former would make you a "regular" at your selected magazines. Especially if your work is accepted, the editors may very soon begin to recognize your name on your submissions. To us, it is always a thrill to have an editor remember us. They are such busy people that it is not too often that they can match a name with a person or recognize the name more than vaguely.

On the other hand, receiving acceptance letters from a variety of publications across the country is also very impressive (it gives you a more diversified writing portfolio). It means that there are quite a few editors who appreciate your work.

You will have to decide for yourself which option would provide the greatest advantage for you. If you would rather become a "regular" somewhere than receive a few acceptances all over, go with the first option. Otherwise, go with the other.

Of course, if you have trouble finding markets that suit your taste, the decision has already been made for you. That is our case. We submit only to a few magazines because they are our favorite markets, and we don't care much for any others.

You have one other major decision to make: Should you submit only one type of literary work or expand to create several types? On the one hand, it is a lot of fun to become an "expert" in one field. Danielle is well known at *Merlyn's Pen* for her puzzles (they have accepted three of them), but not for anything else. *Creative Kids* also proclaimed both of us "game-masters" when they printed our puzzles in *Brain Twisters!* On the other hand, becoming a jack-of-all-writing-trades can be a lot of fun and impressive as well — not to mention it increases your chances for more bylines. If you submit only poems, for example, and your best market has a backlog, the river of acceptances will run dry. However, if you create all kinds of works you could simply shift your focus to something else for a while to compensate. Most importantly, consider what you can do well. Don't force yourself to write poetry if you don't know the first thing about doing it. Create and submit whatever you are good at. As always, the final decisions are yours (see also "The Write Tips" section).

Don't Let Your Manuscripts Get Lost in the Files

Although you may not realize it, keeping good records of your submissions is one of the most important factors in the writing business, especially if you submit a lot of works to different publications. Many good record-keeping systems exist. You must be certain to choose one that makes sense to you and that you can and will easily keep up with. Below are a few suggestions, although if you have your own ideas you can use them as well.

One method incorporates a small hardcover ledger book with lined pages and columns, like the type adults may use for money management. You could label the columns on each page with date sent, title of manuscript, the date that a reply can be expected, the date that it arrives, and whether the manuscript was accepted or rejected. In case of an acceptance, you might have columns for the date that a complimentary copy can be expected and the date that it arrives. By keeping these records, you would know each manuscript's age, whether or not it was accepted, and when you can expect to receive correspondence in the mail. This includes both responses and complimentary copies. You would know which publication a work was sent to according to the page its record is on. (Within the book you could designate certain pages for the records relating to each individual publication you regularly submit to.) By knowing the publication you sent a work to, you would know whether or not you still own rights to it. This might help you determine which works you can submit to other publications.

Another system of record-keeping involves index cards. Give each submitted piece its own card. Include on each card information such as when and where the work was submitted, when you received a reply, whether it was an acceptance or a

rejection, etc. You may also note anything out of the ordinary, such as cash payment. You can keep your cards in a small file box in alphabetical order by title of work or by the publication that each work is sent to.

Also, consider the file cabinet option. This method involves many, many file folders. Label each folder with the title of one of your pieces and fill it with submission information about that piece, plus a copy of the piece if you wish. Then put the folders in a large file box or file cabinet.

You could also organize your information using a bulletin board, if you have one. Write your information on index cards or slips of paper and tack them onto the board alphabetically in rows or columns.

A database is a very helpful method of organizing submission information. This sort of computer program is set up like a large chart, and you can type your information into it. If you are familiar with databases, be sure to consider this option. If not, you may wish to find out more about this system of record-keeping before considering it for yourself. Ask your parents what they know about databases or check your local library or school for information. If you buy a database program, information on how to use it will come with the software.

Please note that if you keep your work stored on a computer disk or hard drive, which is a very good idea, you may also find it beneficial to write down the file in which you've stored each manuscript. When you've written many things, you might forget what file each piece has been stored in, and it can take forever to look through all of the files.

Some people might say that file cabinets take up too much room; others would claim that index card boxes and ledger books are easy to misplace because they are so small. Databases may be convenient for some and confusing to others. Once again, whatever works best for you is fine. All systems keep basically the same information, only in different forms. Be creative; you may even invent your very own record-keeping system.

"OK," you might be thinking. "That's all fine and dandy, but there's one more thing: what do I do with the rest of my submission stuff?" It's true that you may soon be swamped in returned SASEs, rejected copies of your manuscripts, acceptance and rejection letters, and guideline sheets. So what should you do with these?

First of all, keeping the returned SASEs is probably not necessary. However, we sometimes do for future reference. (If we forget to record submission information immediately after receiving responses and fail to remember the information later, we can look at the postmark dates to see when we received our replies. Once we have updated our records fully, we throw the SASEs away). If you send somewhere for guidelines and the envelope comes back "Return to Sender," you may want to keep it. Then you'll remember later on that the publication went out of business or moved. That way you won't accidentally waste paper, envelopes, and stamps sending another guideline request or submission to the same address.

You could throw away rejected copies of your manuscripts as well, unless the editor wrote revision suggestions on them. After all, you can't resubmit an old, folded, or worn copy of your manuscript (see "Writing is a Profession — Act Professional").

You should definitely keep your response letters, especially the acceptance letters. (That way you can mail copies of them to your grandparents or other proud relatives or show them to your friends to prove that you really are having your work published. Also, if you wait for more than a year to see your work in print and fear that the editor has lost your accepted work or does not remember that it was accepted, you can send a copy of the letter as proof of acceptance. Sometimes when an editor is replaced, the new editor is unsure of the status of unpublished work sitting in the office.) These letters may also become an important part of your record system. You can put them in a folder or binder. If you're very cautious (or simply keep everything) and have chosen not to dispose of your SASEs, you may choose to leave the letters inside the envelopes they came in. Keep your rejection letters, too. Most published authors proudly display their "reject file." It's a testament to how much work you've done.

The guidelines are another matter. Of course you must keep these. Not long ago our guidelines were scattered about the house, and it seemed we could never find the ones we were looking for. To solve this problem, we recently stapled ours as necessary, hole-punched them, and compiled them all into one large black binder.

Do what works for you. Here we have recommended that you do what works best for us. If you don't like what we have suggested, don't do it. For example, if you want to keep everything, do so. Whatever you decide to keep as far as submission items, we suggest that you put it in a desk drawer, file box, or file cabinet. If it will fit, put your record-keeping stuff in there as well.

The Grim Realities of Publication

Regardless of your age, rejection is likely to plague your writing "career." *Look Homeward Angel* by Thomas Wolfe was rejected more than 30 times. However, when it was finally published, it sold hundreds of thousands of copies! Even our own submissions can be used as an example. Between the two of us we've made some 100 submissions, and have only 20 some acceptances to show for it.

But we keep trying.

Especially in the beginning, rejection often comes more frequently than acceptance. We don't say this to discourage you; it just comes with the territory. Keep at it though. Most professional authors are very proud of a thick rejection file. Also, there is the possibility of receiving an acceptance the first time you submit something. Jessica did just that, to her surprise, but it still proves the point.

Never assume that you have failed because you received a rejection. The 20 acceptances we have seem few compared to a staggering 100 submissions, but that doesn't make us bad writers. Rejections can be the result of lots of things. Perhaps your work did not fit the style or subject matter of the publication you sent it to. Also, if you write several different kinds of things, send some of each kind to each magazine. For instance, if you write fiction and nonfiction, don't send all of your fiction to a magazine and none of the nonfiction. There is always a chance that the editor has an eye out for nonfiction, but if you don't send any, he or she won't have a chance to consider your work. Maybe the editors just accepted some similar work, or have an extensive backlog. Never think "I'm not good enough" or "I'm a failure." All work can use a little improvement, but that doesn't necessarily mean you wrote your manuscript badly. Never think that just because an editor rejected one of your manuscripts he or she will reject all of them. Perseverance pays off. Also, always remember that following guidelines and studying the contents and needs of a publication boost your chances of acceptance.

Rejection isn't the only frustrating aspect of writing; there is also a good deal of waiting involved. As far as we can tell, sending work to publications involves more waiting than anything else. Responses often take up to three months. You should always wait at least two months before sending a follow-up letter. Never call an editor on the phone to discuss your work (see "Writing is a Profession — Act Professional!). He or she will not have your work available to discuss and it will not improve your chances of being published.

One of the magazines that we've sent work to, *Merlyn's Pen*, receives 15,000 submissions per year. Not only does that mean waiting around 10 weeks for a reply, but it also means reduced chances of acceptance. *Merlyn's Pen* publishes no more than 150 manuscripts per year. You may think that with so few acceptances they'll never want your work, but there is always a chance. If you have faith in your talents and your manuscript, and you have researched the publication's needs and studied its guidelines, it's worth a shot. If you don't have confidence in the ability of your work to be accepted at *Merlyn's Pen* or some other magazine, either edit until you do or pick a publication that you think will like your work better.

Waiting involves not only responses but also the sending and receiving of copies. Should your work be accepted, most magazines send you a free copy of the issue in which your work appears, and this takes a great deal of time.

Although it will be impossible for you to escape the problems above, there is one problem that you can escape: getting swindled. There are contests that will require you to send money in order to receive a prize, or buy a copy of an anthology in order to have your work published in it. Beware of these. Read all notices and letters very carefully. Jessica once had a problem with this. Although she was not required to order a copy of an anthology in order to be published in it, she wanted one. As always, she finds it frustrating not to have copies of everything her work appears in. Unfortunately, the anthology cost her $60, and that was a discount price. After seeing it, she realized that the accomplishment in receiving the acceptance was hardly that at all. Several hundred people had work accepted for publication in it, and all of the poems were crammed together as if they were worthless. It was very disappointing.

On a different note, if your accepted piece requires extensive editing, the editor may ask you to revise the work yourself. If the editor gives any specific instructions, you should follow his or her advice. You must follow the advice as far as grammar, spelling, and punctuation (unless he or she made a very obvious error) as well as advice for rewording phrases and sentences to make them less awkward. After all, the editor has been around a lot longer than you, has most likely received a formal education in grammar and writing, and is more experienced. However, if the editor suggests content revisions and major changes that you are strongly against or wish to modify, contact the editor.

You could write a letter for the editor's convenience, but this would not enable you to have an active discussion over the matter. The revisions need to be made quickly, also, and communication by letter is slow. Look at your situation closely and weigh the matter, then decide between writing to and calling the editor (see "Writing is a Profession — Act Professional!").

Discuss with the editor the matter at hand; suggest compromises but don't demand anything. Being rude will get you nowhere. Once you reach an agreement, stick with it. Do the best you can and send the work back in as soon as possible.

More than likely, however, if your piece was accepted at all, the necessary revising can be done by the editor without too much difficulty. You may be shocked when you see your work in print. Sometimes published work undergoes content revisions drastic enough that the author can tell at a glance that his or her work was changed. Many young authors are disappointed with the revisions merely because they wanted their work to be accepted for what is was, not what it could become. They wanted their work to be kept just the same. Some feel a slight lowering of confidence when they find that their work "wasn't quite good enough" to be published as it was written. A few may even hate the specific changes, feeling that these made the manuscript worse. Don't let revision discourage you, however. It happens to even the best authors. The editor is experienced; he or she makes changes to your piece to make it more clear for the readers, who might then like your work better. Besides, most children's magazine editors make a conscious effort to "preserve" accepted work. Your work should remain as much like its original version as possible. More than likely the basic idea of the piece or the basic story line will not be tampered with.

How to Teach an Old Manuscript New Tricks

By the time you get to be an experienced writer, your works of years ago may embarrass you, but they shouldn't. These works were probably good for a person of your age and level when you wrote them. Even so, you may find them to be less than acceptable in comparison to your more current work. For example, read the poem below:

Fly Swatting Relief
By Danielle Dunn

A fly was buzzing around my knee,
So I picked up the fly swatter and slapped it with glee,
And then another one came along,
Buzzing, buzzing, singing its song.

I threw back my arm and slapped him as well,
Feeling, all the while, really swell,
Because no doubt about it, even when mad,
Killing a bug can make anyone glad.

Danielle wrote this poem at the age of 12. For that age level, and at the time, having had little experience, she felt it was pretty good. However, by now she is so embarrassed about it that she barely agreed to include it as an example! It was never published in a magazine. Below is another poem, by the same author, written just one year later when she was 13.

Hunt of the Lioness
By Danielle Dunn

The lioness moved stealthily
Patiently
Quiet as a mouse
Through the tall flax-colored grass
Of the Serengeti Plains in Africa
Her golden brown fur
Blending in with the grass
Shielding her from sight.

Her eyes focused
On the gazelle
Her prey.

She thought of the gazelle
Food
Nothing else.
She and the gazelle alone existed.
Her long tail twitched
She moved closer
Closer to the gazelle
Eyes glinting
Her mouth beginning to water.

Patiently
She stepped ever closer ...
He saw her
Fled
To escape from Death.

The lioness bolted
Across the plains
After him.
The gazelle, weak, ran

Ran feebly.

Stumbling
He had no chance.

In seconds
The lioness caught up with him
Sprang halfway onto his back
Sank her teeth
Into his throat
Dragged him down
To the ground.

The gazelle struggled.
The lioness held her grip on his throat.
Finally he stopped struggling,
Lay still.
Success at last.

She and her family could eat.

This poem, written only one year later, is noticeably more sophisticated. Having submitted many works to magazines during the year's difference, Danielle had gained experience in getting her work published, as well as in writing itself. Perhaps submitting work to publications not only raises self-esteem, but improves writing technique more quickly than just practicing. Editors give advice, and getting accepted encourages people to keep improving their work sometimes more than sheer desire to write does.

Improvements in your technique can serve another purpose besides helping you to write new and better manuscripts; it can help you improve old ones. Remember the first section of this book where we told you to keep copies of your work? Well, here's another reason why you should. You can look back in your files and edit your old, unpublished works to suit your new technique and style.

If you keep good records, you can pull up, on your computer, any unpublished works or published ones that you still have rights to. Then you can edit them. Who knows? You just might gain an acceptance on a manuscript you wrote a few years ago when you couldn't before. Or, if the work was published before, you can have it published again elsewhere depending on the original magazine's rights agreement.

A portfolio can help you track your progress from "amateur" to "professional." Using this, you may someday look back at your work and see how much your writing improved from year to year. In your portfolio, keep copies of several of your pieces, including stories, poems, and/or whatever else you may write, from year to year. Keep the pieces in chronological order by date created; put your oldest pieces at the front and your most recent at the back. You may keep them in a folder, binder, etc., whatever works best for you (there's that famous line again!). This way you may open your portfolio 20 years from now and read it like a book from beginning to end, seeing your work improve right before your eyes! You could also use it as a reference more frequently. For example, you might look through it every few months or once a year and from it determine if your writing is improving as quickly and as much as you want it to. If it does not appear to be getting any better, you may consider options such as taking a writing course in order to improve the quality of your submissions and keep yourself up-to-date in the world of publishing.

In addition to keeping a portfolio, you may wish to keep a journal to describe your progress in writing and publishing. Make note of each of your acceptances and the excitement that accompanies them. Most importantly describe your feelings as you progress through your writing career. A portfolio of written pieces cannot express your elation at acceptance and publication or your fear of rejection.

Later you could read your journal for pleasure to see how far you've come and how you handled the trials, tribulations, and excitement of the publishing process. You could also use your journal in some of your other writings.

As we wrote this book, we created journals describing our feelings, anxieties, and expectations for the book. We included these journals in portfolios we each made. The portfolios, with letters and copies of the manuscript at each stage of revision, show the progress of our book through the publishing process. In the future and even now we will both enjoy these vivid depictions of the progress of our first major publication.

Alternative Publishing

The most straightforward way for a person living in the U.S. to see work in print is to submit it to a national, professional U.S. magazine or book press. This is also one of the most difficult. There are alternatives. These may be appealing for a beginner or a more experienced young writer looking for a change.

Self-publishing is paying to have your work printed by a print shop or printing it yourself. It can also be printing a school newspaper or yearbook, or using a computer to desktop-publish works and distribute them to neighbors.

This is an option. However, be forewarned that you will most likely lose money this way. It's hard to make a profit when you have to pay for something to be printed in the first place, even if all you spend is money for photocopies.

Also, self-publishing can be ultimately self-indulgent. It may be a put down against you because other people may naturally think that your work wasn't "good enough" to be published by a real publisher. They may assume that you were desperate to see your work in print and wouldn't wait to be published for real (that's self-indulgent). This impatience is not a good reason to self-publish. If that would be your one and only reason, we suggest you not do it.

Self-indulgence isn't always the case. Your work is probably very good and you may self-publish a collection of previously published works for the fun of it.

You may print your own work with a desktop publishing program and sell it for practice or along with submitting work to professional magazines. School publications are also nice to put your works into so that your peers can see them.

You are strongly encouraged, however, to submit your work to national magazines for children. The feeling you get from receiving an acceptance by one of these publications can be much more fulfilling than self-publishing. When adult editors think your work is really good, it must be really good!

Vanity or subsidy publishing is another option. It is much like self-publishing because you pay to have it done; however, the editing and production are all handled for you. The advertisements for these publishers always sound so wonderful. They talk about printing beautiful, wonderful books by talented people and describe in detail the production and marketing process that will take place. Then they encourage you to send your work, listing names of other "famous" authors who did in order to convince you that it's a good idea. Unfortunately, the real point is often avoided: you pay for everything. Sometimes they even beat about the bush by claiming that the fees are "reasonable." They avoid estimating the total bill. Five hundred dollars or more isn't uncommon at all in vanity publishing; no wonder they don't want to admit it! Business would be ruined!

Although this is an alternative form of publishing, it's not an advisable one. When you send in your work, the editors will probably write back saying that they loved it, lavishing praise on you as a great author. You may be good, but the praise is most often exaggerated and misleading. The editors simply say these wonderful things, whether they are true or not, to get your money. It's not an honest appraisal of your work.

There is nothing illegal about subsidy or vanity publishing. However, the ultimate feeling you'll get from it is feeling cheated, not elated. The only advantage is seeing your work in print, but that's hardly an advantage at all when it wasn't even done by a reputable publisher. Besides, what's the point in having your work published if no one will see it?

Despite what they say, the marketing done by these presses is often very poor or nonexistent. Your money covers production and profit; why would the publisher care about marketing your book if he doesn't need the money from selling it to recover costs? Your book will most likely sit in a warehouse (see also "The Big Don'ts of Publishing").

Local, religious, and school publications, however, are perfectly accessible and can make very good markets for your work. For example, you might put some of your stories or other works in a church newsletter or other local newspaper. These markets are too localized to be listed in our directory; there is no way a writer in Virginia would want to send something to a church newsletter in Sugar Land, Texas, for instance. Depending on where you live and what your religion is, you can probably find some local or religious markets for yourself. You may stumble across an ad in the paper or ask some people you know about these markets. There are some other market guides that do list more localized and some religious publications.

Also, many schools have student journalism staffs that publish school newsletters and write the yearbook. See what you can find out about becoming part of the staff or submitting your work as a freelancer. Also, look at the list of other references found in the back of this book.

Foreign markets can also be very appealing. Many great contests and magazines are sponsored or published in Canada, for example. However, making submissions to a foreign country will require IRCs (International Reply Coupons). These must be enclosed with your SASE rather than U.S. postage stamps. A Canadian editor can't send a response to you with a U.S. stamp, just as you couldn't send anything to him or her with a Canadian stamp.

IRCs can be used by a foreign publisher to purchase the necessary stamps which can then be placed on your SASE and mailed. Use U.S. stamps on your outer envelope to send the work to the foreign country (ask at the post office how many; mailing to foreign countries always costs more). Be sure to enclose IRCs for the editor's use (again ask at the post office how many).

The last alternative (unless you have any more ideas) is publishing through the computer. On-line or bulletin board services can allow you to "post" your work in a network. Other people can then access your work on the computer and read it on the screen if and when they want to. KidPub in the Internet offers this "publishing" service, for example.

The Big Don'ts of Publishing

Publishing holds many opportunities in store for you. Most of them are excellent, but there are a few that you should avoid:

Acting like a Know-it-all. Magazine editors carry with them an expertise in grammar, publishing, editing, and often years of experience. It would be a serious mistake for you to completely disregard an editor's advice or any suggestions for manuscript revisions. If an editor rejects your manuscript but suggests how you can make it better, you should strongly consider making the changes and resubmitting the manuscript to the same publication or elsewhere. You may choose never to submit the work again, but if you do resubmit it, be sure to make the editor's suggested changes. Never resubmit the work to the same publication without making these changes because you will guarantee yourself a rejection. Likewise, if your manuscript is accepted, and the editor asks you to revise it, you should pretty much follow the suggestions, unless the editor accidentally makes a definite grammatical error (see "The Grim Realities of Publication").

Sometimes in their guidelines editors will also give tips or advice on how to submit to their publication. Do not skip over this. Be sure to read it thoroughly and pay heed to what it says.

Entering a contest before studying all the facts. Suppose you come across a contest that you would like to enter. The fee is a little high, but you are willing to spend the money. So you jump in and send out your entry. Unfortunately, you notice later that this is a national contest open to all ages, has a pretty substantial prize, and is sponsored by a popular or well-known organization or publication. (These factors would make it a very popular contest.) Suddenly it hits you that this contest will have a very large number of entrants, some of them adults. Adults are more likely to have their work win because they may have been writing a lot longer and may be a lot better at it. You have a very slim chance of winning, and you just spent a substantial amount of cash on your entry!

You must read the contest information very carefully. You may find that this contest has a very high entry fee and gives you a very slim chance of winning. Now that you at least know, you can consider this risky situation carefully. Normally, submitting to such a contest is little more than throwing your money away.

However, if you have the money to spare and the contest is a little more localized (generally meaning that it has fewer entrants), especially if it is open only to young people, go for it! As long as you have confidence in your work and a good chance to win, it may be worth the cash.

Note: Please do not think that a contest judging fee is equivalent to paying for publication (see vanity publishing). The judging fee is usually small and is used to pay the contest judges and cover the prize money. Publication of winning manuscripts is usually paid for by the sale of the collection or work. Entry fees are also very common, while most presses don't charge authors for publication; only vanity presses do this.

Overconfidence. This is setting yourself up for disappointment. For example, some writers have their first submitted work accepted. They may then think that they will never have work rejected and that their writing careers will be peaches and cream for the rest of their lives. Forget it! All writers have to face rejection once in a while. Overconfidence is also sending work to *Ladies Home Journal* or *Reader's Digest* and expecting to have your work published. Even adults don't often think it's easy to get their manuscripts accepted by those publications. The chances are even slimmer for a child or teenager. Set realistic goals. One of Jessica's is to have at least three puzzles published in *Merlyn's Pen*. Danielle achieved this goal, and

Jessica looks forward to doing the same. That is realistic; expecting to write a string of bestsellers before you are 25 is not. Entering contests with stiff competition, usually including adults, also often shows overconfidence.

Lack of confidence. This is also dangerous and can just as easily jeopardize your writing career. Some young writers, upon receiving their first rejection slip, deem themselves failures and give up making submissions. This is a big mistake. If every writer on this Earth did that, there would be no writers. Besides, just because an editor rejects your work doesn't mean he or she is rejecting you. You can always make another submission. Remember this.

Some writers have a very low level of confidence in their work itself. An example would be the kind of writer who sits at a typewriter with his head in his hands surrounded by crumpled up balls of paper. You should never be disappointed by everything you write. (Every writer will sometimes look at work she's written and think, "This is really bad!" but don't think this too often.)

Write a few pieces, select your best work, and submit it. It's always worth a shot. (If you have no self-confidence it will probably also show in your writing! Be careful.)

Vanity / Subsidy Publishing. This is one example of alternative publishing that seems far too good to be true, and is. Basically, this is paying to see your work in print, usually books. It is best to have work published because an editor really feels it deserves recognition, not because a press is asking for bribes in order to print work. The money you pay will cover profit and the cost of production. Because the press will then have all the money it needs, it won't put out a very good effort to market your work. Ultimately you will have thrown away your money on a book almost no one will ever see (see also "Alternative Publishing"). Furthermore, you will not benefit from professional editing or marketing of your work.

The Writing Life

Finding My Place in the Publishing World

I can't remember everything about how I got started writing, since I didn't always keep the best of records. However, I have recorded the most important things in my memory.

For one thing, my very first submission was a success. The editors at *Creative Kids* accepted my first poem. This I say as an example, to prove to you that it can happen. Some people think it's an unwritten law that a young writer must submit 20 manuscripts to magazines before the editors even look at the person's work with interest. As in my case, this is not necessarily so. Have faith in yourself. You may get an acceptance on the first try, or you may not. Still, that doesn't mean you have to wait years.

I think almost everything involved with writing is terrific. I love getting acceptances, complimentary copies, advice so that I can improve my work, and I especially like having knowledge of the field. Although I hardly know anything about national publications and adult freelancing, I enjoy knowing what I'm doing when I submit my work to smaller magazines. It's a great hobby, and a great way of raising self-esteem when you succeed. Typing, submitting, and working on manuscripts can cause some stress, but in the end the acceptance makes up for it.

The worst two things about writing and submitting work are waiting and rejections. Rejections hurt anybody.

Waiting is almost as bad. One summer I was bored a lot, and so I greatly looked forward to getting the mail. Most days, as I expected, I didn't get anything. The longer I was forced to wait between replies, the more aggravating it became. Getting a response at all always delighted me, whether it was an acceptance or a rejection. Even though rejections aren't the best, there is a bright side to them: I can follow any advice given by the editor and then resubmit the work to the same publication or a new one for another shot at an acceptance. Then I still have something out in the mail for which I can look forward to a reply.

A system that I've developed just recently helps me to make sure that I can always look forward to getting something in the mail. I always make sure that I have at least two submissions out, and every time I get a reply I look in my records to see if I've dropped below that mark. If I have, I make another submission as soon as possible to catch up. This may be a new manuscript, or I may submit a rejected manuscript to the same publication or a different one, depending upon whether or not I did any editing. For example, if I made any changes to the manuscript I could send it back to the same publication. If the editor didn't suggest editing and resubmitting it, I could send it somewhere else.

As far as the rest of the story goes, what can I say? Most of the experience of writing isn't very easy to explain. Even though you may find that hard to believe now, I think you'll know what I'm talking about when you get started. There is so much to it that I can't tell you everything. You'll just have to discover the rest for yourself.

—*Jessica Dunn*

My Life in Writing

It all began with boredom. As far back as I can remember I've enjoyed writing. After a while, however, the whole thing started to bore me. I never did anything with my stories and poems; I just wrote them and then lost them or threw them away. When it occurred to me to try to get my work published, I dove right into the project. For more than a month, I went to the public library with my sister Jessica two and three days a week, searching for just the right markets. Through this effort, and from a list I received at a conference, I learned about *Stone Soup*, *Merlyn's Pen*, and *Creative Kids*. Since 1992, when I started, I have received 15 acceptance letters from various magazines, including the above with the exception of *Stone Soup*. I started off writing stories and poems. Somewhere along the line, however, I decided to submit puzzles for publication, also. Six of my 15 acceptances are puzzles and they were all accepted in one summer (two at *Creative Kids* which also appeared in two books by the same publisher, and three at *Merlyn's Pen*)! Of course I feel great, and I'm still going strong! By the way, 15 acceptances may not sound like much for three years, but it takes several months for a publication to reply to one submission!

There's something else I should tell you about. Not all of my accepted manuscripts have been published yet. That's because the time period between acceptance and publication in a magazine may be up to a year or more! This time period is called lead time. No matter how quickly they publish my work, it really is a long time to wait.

I wish you luck in getting accepted at magazines. Hopefully you'll be even more successful than us. All you have to do is WRITE!

—Danielle Dunn

Appendix

Glossary

all rights: rights situation in which a magazine that publishes one's work owns that work, even from the moment of acceptance. You, then, no longer have the right to submit that article to other magazines or publications unless you get permission from the original publisher of your work. You must sign a form for this. If you do not sign anything, then you retain copyright, no matter what, even if you are paid.

backlog: large collection of a certain type of literary manuscript, such as poems, that are all waiting to be published. For example, when a publication has enough poems to fill its issues for a year or so, it usually stops accepting them until the backlog is reduced.

byline: line below the title of a manuscript where the author's name is printed. Sometimes authors are said to be "hungry for a byline," which means "eager to see your work in print."

complimentary copy: free copy of an issue of a magazine in which an author's work appears. It is automatically sent to the author at the magazine's expense if offered. Also known as contributors' copies.

copyright: Legal protection of an author's published work against plagiarism or unauthorized publication of the work. An author automatically owns the copyright unless it is expressly granted to another entity in writing.

First North American rights: rights situation in which a magazine requests rights to be the first North American publisher of a work. Most publications in the U.S. use this type of agreement. The work may be previously unpublished or published in Europe, Asia, or another part of the world. After publication, the creator or author is free to submit it elsewhere.

First time rights: rights requested by a publication under the agreement that the work will be published by that publication once and for the first time in the world.

genre: a type or style of literature. For example, horror is a fiction genre and self-help is a nonfiction genre. Genre has a confusing pronunciation; it is (zhaanra).

lead time: period of time during which a magazine plans the issue in which an accepted work will appear. This period of time separates the time of acceptance from the time of publication of said work. Lead times usually run from three months to even a year or more.

masthead: list of members of a publication's staff, found in the front of any issue of a magazine. This is one place to look for an editor's name and address before making a submission (see "Letter and Manuscript Formats"). Be sure to look at the most recent issue. This is sometimes confused with the magazine's logo or title. That is called the flag.

multiple submission: the submission of more than one article in the same envelope and to the same publication.

one time use rights: rights situation that gives a magazine the right to publish a work only one time. The magazine would then have to receive permission from the author and give credit and compensation to him or her if the magazine wanted to reuse it.

plagiarism: copying a work or part of a work written by another person, calling it your own, and then using it for personal profit or achievement.

reprint rights: rights given to a publication usually along with first time rights. They give the publication the right to reprint the work in anthologies or other types of publications by the same publisher.

rights: states who owns and has rights to a published work, either the publisher or the author.

SASE (self-addressed stamped envelope): an envelope in which a publication will send a reply to an author. The return address is that of the publication and the address in the middle is that of the author. Because the author is the one to write on the envelope, it is labeled as being self-addressed. Don't forget to put on a stamp or two, and never seal the envelope.

simultaneous submission: the submission of one article to more than one publication at the same time.

Directory of Publications and Contests

This directory contains several magazine publishers, book publishers, and contest sponsors, as well as brief information about each company and contest. As always, it will be necessary to send for guidelines. However, the information here will help you to decide, even before sending out guideline requests, which publications and contests you might like to send your work to. It is our hope that you will enjoy writing for the following, as they include a few of our favorites.

Magazines

The Apprentice Writer
c/o Gary Fincke
Susquehanna University
Selinsgrove, PA 17870

Contributors: grades 9-12
Publishes: fiction, poetry, essays, drama, journalism-features/interviews, photos, and art
Responds on May 5 each year (published annually)
First time use rights; rights revert back to author after publication
Complimentary copy is sent

Common mistakes to avoid: sending work that is too long; failing to include name and address; querying without sending an SASE
Editor: Gary Fincke
Sample copy: $2.50

Boodle: By Kids, For Kids
P.O. Box 1049
Portland, IN 47371

Ph. #: (219) 726-8141
Contributors: Kids
Publishes: artwork, puzzles, mazes, stories, poetry
Responds in 6 - 8 weeks
Author retains copyright after publication; magazine takes first time rights
Two complimentary copies are sent
Common mistakes to avoid: writing depressing work about illness and death; submitting very long stories, stories with long-winded conversations, or poems with forced rhyme; writing work that is too similar to work previously printed
Editor: Mavis Catalfio
Sample Copy: $2.50

Boomerang!
13366 Pescadero Road, Box 261
La Honda, CA 94020

Note: this is an audiomagazine, published on cassette tapes
Ph.#: (800) 333-7858 or (415) 747-0978
Contributors: ages 6-12
Publishes: book reviews, letters, stories, interviews
Responds in 1 month

Rights are variable, usually all rights; may submit work
elsewhere if submitted on cassette tape or if printed in the insert accompanying the audiocassette
A complimentary copy is sent
Work most needed: jokes, accomplishments, historical
milestones, kids in the news, funny parent stories,
fake commercials, editorials, prefers submissions
already on tape
Common mistakes to avoid: trying to sound like an adult
Editors: David Strom, Amie Breed
Sample copy: $3 postage

Creative Kids Magazine
P.O. Box 8813
Waco, TX 76714-8813

Ph. #: (817) 756-3337
Contributors: Ages 8-14
Publishes: cartoons, songs, stories, puzzles, photographs, art-
work, games, activities, editorials, articles
Responds in 8 weeks
Magazine holds reprint rights; author retains copyright
A complimentary copy is sent; no cash payment
Work most needed: art and photos, editorials
Common mistakes to avoid: forgetting SASE, sending
simultaneous or multiple submissions
Managing Editor: Libby Lindsey
Sample copy: $3.75

Creative With Words
P.O. Box 223226
Carmel, CA 93922

Contributors: Kids and sometimes adults
Publishes: poetry, prose, other writings, computer art, and

folkloristic tales

Responds in 2 months

Author retains copyright; takes one time use rights; however, if work is sent elsewhere, CWW gets a byline for publishing first

No complimentary copy; copy can be purchased at 20% discount

Work most needed: any work that follows the theme list

Common mistakes to avoid: not following guidelines, not following theme list, not including an SASE

Editor-in-chief: Brigitta Geltrich Staff editor: Bert Hower

Sample Copy: $5

Note: Send for guidelines, theme list, and deadlines

Highlights for Children
803 Church Streets
Honesdale, PA 18431

Ph. #: (717) 253-1080

Contributors: any age

Publishes: stories, poems, drawings, riddles, jokes, tongue twisters, craft ideas, and finger/action plays

Responds in 6 weeks

Magazine owns copyright; takes all rights and copyright

Complimentary copies are sent

Work most needed: great fiction, accessible nonfiction

Common mistakes to avoid: underestimating kids' interests and abilities

Submissions Editor: Beth Troop

Sample copy: $2.95

Note: under 15, no payment; does not guarantee publication

Ink Blot Newsletter
901 Day Road
Saginaw, Michigan 48609

Contributors: Any age
Publishes: articles, short stories, short fillers, poetry, and
    artwork
Responds in 2 to 4 months
Author retains copyright, one time rights used
A complimentary copy is sent
Work most needed: poetry
Common mistakes to avoid: not including an SASE; not
    including age, grade, and name of school
Editor: Margaret Larkin
Sample copy: $1.00 and SASE
Note: Write for theme list and deadlines; address listed is
    temporary

Kid's Korner Newsletter
P.O. Box 413
Joaquin, TX 75954

Contributors: ages 6-17
Publishes: fiction, nonfiction, artwork
Editor: Marcella Simmons

Merlyn's Pen Magazine
The National Magazines of Student Writing, Middle
    School and High School editions
P.O. Box 1058
E. Greenwich, RI 02818

Ph. # : (800) 247-2027
Contributors: Grades 6-12
Publishes: short stories, poems, essays, plays, art, puzzles
    (middle school edition only), games, and photogra-
    phy
Responds in 10 weeks
MP owns copyright after publication and all rights

Three complimentary copies are sent, plus payment
Work most needed: more artwork; more reviews of movies, books, and work published in the magazine
Mistakes to avoid: not following the guidelines and not writing from your own experience, about things you know
Editor: Christine Lord
Sample Copy: free
Note: No SASE (unless asking for guidelines), send shipping and handling fee, form cover sheet (send for this)

Skipping Stones
P.O. Box 3939
Eugene, OR 97403-0939

Ph. #: (503) 342-4956
Contributors: all ages
Publishes: artwork, photos, games, quizzes, activities, stories, poems, riddles, pen pals, letters; also takes work in foreign languages with English translation
Responds in 3 months
Magazine holds first serial rights and reprint rights, but authors retain copyright and may submit work elsewhere after publication
Complimentary copy is sent
Work most needed: more nonfiction, more stories of personal experiences, and especially work with multicultural themes; they get plenty of poetry, but you can send it
Common mistakes to avoid: sending material with an inappropriate subject, sending works that are too long
Editor: Arun Toke
Sample Copy: $5

Spring Tides
Savannah Country Day Lower School
824 Stillwood Road
Savannah, GA 31419-2643

Ph. #: (912) 925-8800
Contributors: Ages 5-12
Publishes: stories and poems with or without illustrations
Responds in 6 months to one year
Rights: one time use rights; author retains copyright
Complimentary copy is sent
Work most needed: fiction and nonfiction
Common mistakes to avoid: not following guidelines
Editor: Connie Houston
Sample Copy: $5

Stone Soup Magazine
P.O. Box 83
Santa Cruz, CA 95063

Ph. #: (408) 426-5557 or (800) 447-4569
Contributors: Ages through 13
Publishes: stories, poems, book reviews, art, plays, just
    about anything by kids
Responds in 4 weeks
Retains the copyright; all rights
Two complimentary copies are sent
Work most needed: good work written by children; nothing
    in particular
Common mistakes to avoid: not sending an SASE (must
    send one for response)
Editor: Gerry Mandel
Sample Copy: $4

Young Voices
P.O. Box 2321
Olympia, WA 98507

Ph. #: (360) 357-4683
Contributors: all young people
Publishes: stories, poems, essays, drawings
Responds in at least 2 months
Rights: one-time
A complimentary copy is sent
Work most needed: quality nonfiction; they have plenty of
poetry
Common mistake to avoid: not revising sufficiently
Editor: Steve Charak
Sample Copy: $4

Book Publishers

Free Spirit Publishing, Inc.
400 First Ave. N., Suite 616
Minneapolis, MN 55401-1730

Ph. #: 1-800-735-7323 for catalog or guidelines, not to dis-
cuss work
Contributors: 14 and up.
Publishes: books on psychology, self-help, how-to, education
Responds in 3-4 months
Takes absolutely all exclusive world rights (you can never
republish it anywhere)
Usually 10 complimentary copies; negotiable
Work most needed: nonfiction books, self-help
Common mistakes to avoid: not researching the types of
books published by Free Spirit
Editorial Assistant: M.E. Salzmann
NOTE: Specify student guidelines when requesting
writer's guidelines

Kopper Bear Press
P.O. Box 19454
Boulder, CO 80308-2454

Contributors: 13-21 years old
Publishes: fiction, nonfiction, short stories, poetry, novels, novellas, essays, etc.
Responds in 6 months
Complimentary copies: negotiable

Raspberry Publication, Inc.
P.O. Box 925
Westerville, OH 43081-6925

Ph. #: (800) 759-7171 or (614) 841-4353
Contributors: Kindergarten through grade 12 or ages 5 through 18
Publishes: books of any length, any topic or genre; poetry or prose form
Responds in at least 2 months
Author retains copyright, rights are on individual contract basis Five copies of published books are sent to authors
Work most needed: mystery, relationship, math-related manuscripts, works from high school and middle school students, anything different
Common mistakes to avoid: grammar and spelling errors; however, never concentrate on these as much as content. Be careful, but look more at content.
Publisher/editor: Susan Schmidt

Tyketoon Young Authors Publishing Company
7417 Douglas Lane
Fort Worth, TX 76180

Ph. #: (817) 581-2876
Contributors: grades 1-8
Publishes: fiction, nonfiction, and poetry picture books
Responds in 3 months

Contests

National Written and Illustrated by ... Awards Contest for
    Students
Landmark Editions, Inc.
1402 Kansas Ave.
Kansas City, MO 64127

Ph. #: (816) 241-4919
Ages: 6-19
Work judged: illustrated novels
Responds on Oct.15 (winners only, notified by phone), oth-
    ers sent back by December
Author retains copyright
Several complimentary copies are offered; negotiated in
    contract
Most needed works: open to anything
Common mistake to avoid: having a strong beginning and
    ending but weak body (middle) in the manuscript
Deadline: May 1 of each year

There are numerous contests not listed here because
they are too subject to change; however they are worth
mentioning. For example, *Creative Kids*, *Merlyn's Pen*, and
Byline all hold various contests off and on. (*Byline* only
publishes winning contest entries by students and other
work by adults; no unsolicited manuscripts are consid-
ered.) In order to know of all of them, however, you would
probably need to subscribe. Otherwise, if and when you get
sample copies from these magazines, take a look through

them for contest listings. If your library subscribes, look through those, too. Keep your eyes open for other notices as well; some contests are listed in local newspapers, for example.

Other Reference Materials

Although we have done our best to sum up what you need to know to be a successful young writer, we haven't said it all. We have not gone into detail about how you can improve your writing skills; instead, take a look at some of these books for professional advice and more markets for your work. You may find the books in the lists below to be of interest.

Write to the following address for a complete listing of books written for writers, noting specifically those listed below:

Writer's Digest Books
1507 Dana Ave.
Cincinnati, OH 45207

28 Biggest Writing Blunders (and how to avoid them), by William Noble; $12.95

29 Most Common Writing Mistakes and How to Avoid Them, by Judy Delton; $9.95

Annual Children's Writer's and Illustrator's Market, edited by Christine Martin; $19.99

Annual Writer's Market, edited by Mark Garvey and Kirsten Holm; $26.99

A Beginner's Guide to Getting Published, 2nd Edition, by the Editors of Writer's Digest Books; hardcover $16.99

Beginning Writer's Answer Book, 5th Edition, by Kirk Polking and editors of Writer's Digest Magazine; hardcover $16.99

Complete Guide to Self-Publishing, by Tom and Marilyn Ross; $18.99

Complete Guide to Writing Fiction, by Barnaby Conrad; $17.95

Essential Software for Writers, by Hy Bender; $24.95

Market Guide for Young Writers, by Kathy Henderson; $16.99

Writer's Book of Checklists, by Scott Edelstein; $16.95

Writing Creative Nonfiction, Theodore A. Reescheney; $15.95

Writing A to Z, edited by Kirk Polking; $19.95

The next two books can be ordered by calling or writing for an order form:

Raspberry Publications, Inc.
P.O. Box 925
Westerville, OH 43086-6925
1-800-759-7171

Young Author's Guide to Writing, by editors of Raspberry Publications, Inc.; $8.95

Young Author's Guide to Publishers, by editors of Raspberry Publications, Inc.; $8.95

Order the following by calling Free Spirit Publishing, Inc. at 1-800-735-7323:

Writing Down the Days, by Lorraine M. Dahlstrom; $12.95

Order the book below by writing to:

Macmillan Publishing Co., Inc.
866 Third Avenue
New York, NY 10022

The Elements of Style, by William Strunk Jr. and E.B. White; $11.95

For the book listed below, write to:

Harper and Row, Publishers
10 East 53rd Street
New York, NY 10022

Writing for Publication, by Clarkson N. Potter; $17.95

To order the book below, write to:

St. Martin's Press
175 Fifth Avenue
New York, NY 10010

How to Be Successfully Published in Magazines, edited by Linda Konner; paperback, $11.95

Note: It is advisable for you to look at your local library first for any of the above books you would like to read. The prices are subject to change at any time should you order one. Also, you should browse around at the library and look for other books on writing and publishing. You may find a few not listed here that would be very helpful to you.

Postage

	1-4 pages	5-9 pages	10-14 pages	15-19 pages
9" x 12" envelope with SASE and manuscript in it	$.55	$.78	$.78	$1.01
6½" x 9½" SASE with manuscript in it (for return trips)	$.55	$.55	$.78	$1.01

The postage chart above approximates how much you need to spend on postage for your submissions. The first column shows the number of pages in your manuscript. For instance, you could send a work to a publication in a 9" x 12" size envelope, with an SASE and a manuscript 1-4 pages long enclosed within it. Then you would look (on the postage chart) down the column that says "1-4 pages." Stop when you reach the first row. Doing this, you would find that in such a situation your postage on the outer envelope would need to be 55 cents. As for the SASEs, these need postage for the return trip from the publication to you with a reply enclosed.

To determine how many stamps your SASE will need, figure out the maximum number of sheets of paper that may be sent in it. Usually the maximum will be the same as the number of pages in your manuscript plus your cover letter and a response letter. Find the number of pages in the second line, then look to the right for the postage. If the maximum total will be between one and four pages, your cost will be $.55.

About the Authors

Danielle and Jessica Dunn are 15-year-old fraternal twins. They are currently freshmen at Dulles High School in Sugar Land, Texas, though they were eighth graders at Dulles Middle School when they wrote this, their first book. They have been writing for publication since 1992 and have had works appear in *Creative Kids*, *Young Authors' Magazine Anthologies*, *Merlyn's Pen*, and a few other publications. Danielle and Jessica are currently working on their third book and enjoy reading and playing viola in the school orchestra. They live with thier parents in Sugar Land, Texas.